FOUNDATIONS OF PHYSICS

ELECTRICITY

by Anita Nahta Amin

pogo

Ideas for Parents and Teachers

Pogo Books let children practice reading informational text while introducing them to nonfiction features such as headings, labels, sidebars, maps, and diagrams, as well as a table of contents, glossary, and index.

Carefully leveled text with a strong photo match offers early fluent readers the support they need to succeed.

Before Reading

- "Walk" through the book and point out the various nonfiction features. Ask the student what purpose each feature serves.
- Look at the glossary together. Read and discuss the words.

Read the Book

- Have the child read the book independently.
- Invite him or her to list questions that arise from reading.

After Reading

- Discuss the child's questions. Talk about how he or she might find answers to those questions.
- Prompt the child to think more. Ask: How do you use electricity? Do you know where the electricity you use comes from?

Pogo Books are published by Jump!
5357 Penn Avenue South
Minneapolis, MN 55419
www.jumplibrary.com

Library of Congress Cataloging-in-Publication Data

Names: Amin, Anita Nahta, author.
Title: Electricity / by Anita Nahta Amin.
Description: Minneapolis: Jump!, Inc., [2022]
Series: Foundations of physics
Includes index. | Audience: Ages 7-10
Identifiers: LCCN 2020054267 (print)
LCCN 2020054268 (ebook)
ISBN 9781636900308 (hardcover)
ISBN 9781636900315 (paperback)
ISBN 9781636900322 (ebook)
Subjects: LCSH: Electricity–Juvenile literature.
Classification: LCC QC527.2 .A45 2022 (print)
LCC QC527.2 (ebook) | DDC 537–dc23
LC record available at https://lccn.loc.gov/2020054267
LC ebook record available at https://lccn.loc.gov/2020054268

Editor: Eliza Leahy
Designer: Michelle Sonnek

Photo Credits: EHStockphoto/Shutterstock, cover, 4; New Africa/Shutterstock, 1; Selin Aydogan/Shutterstock, 3; Zoomik/Shutterstock, 5; Bamidor/Shutterstock, 6; Juan Roballo/Shutterstock, 7; Photos by Brook Rieman/Getty, 8-9; Eshma/Shutterstock, 10-11; indianstockimages/Shutterstock, 12-13; Peteri/Shutterstock, 14; pedrosala/Shutterstock, 15; sarintra chimphoolsuk/Shutterstock, 16-17; Shutterstock, 18-19; eyes on him/Shutterstock, 20-21; Yellow Cat/Shutterstock, 23.

Printed in the United States of America at Corporate Graphics in North Mankato, Minnesota.

TABLE OF CONTENTS

CHAPTER 1

POWER UP!

You try to turn on the TV. But it won't turn on. It is unplugged. You plug it into the wall outlet. Now the TV works!

Electricity is all around us. Electronics, like TVs, run on it. So do many **appliances**. Electricity turns on lights. It powers laptops and cell phones.

CHAPTER 2

HOW DOES ELECTRICITY WORK?

We cannot see **electrons**. But we can see what they do. They turn on TVs and lights. They make electricity!

Electrons are parts of **atoms**. We cannot see them. But they make up all things. This includes you!

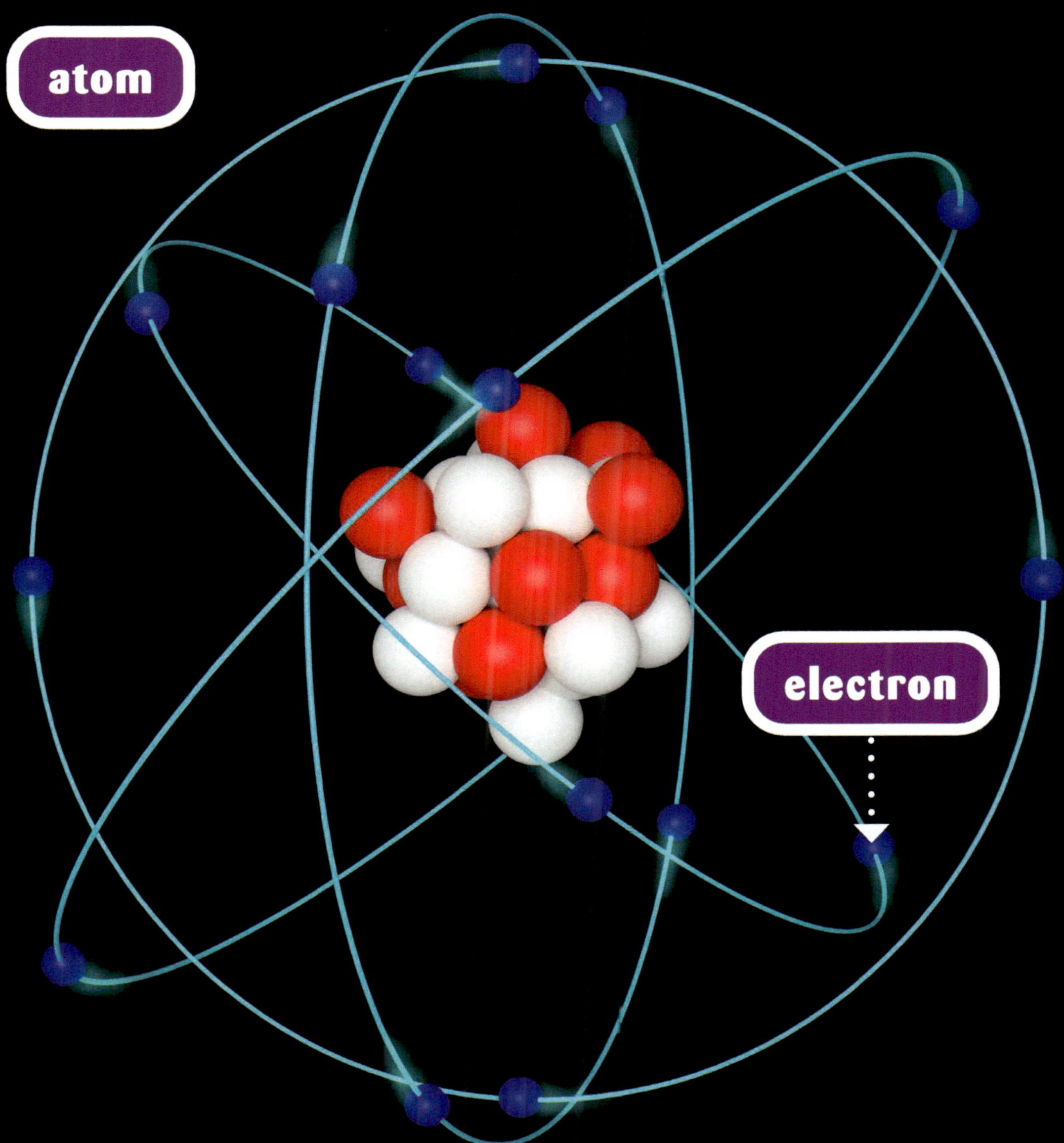

Each electron has a **charge**. When two things rub together, one often gives electrons to the other. Static electricity is created when objects have unbalanced charges.

Some things, like hair, give up electrons. Other things, like wool, take them. You see this when you take off your hat. Does your hair stand up? The hat took electrons from your hair!

DID YOU KNOW?

When you touch something, such as a doorknob, it might take charge from you. This can feel like a shock!

static
electricity

Lightning is another example of static electricity. It occurs when ice and water bump together in a cloud. Ice gives electrons to the water. A flash of static electricity fills the sky!

DID YOU KNOW?

Many objects can keep us safe in storms. Cars, planes, and buildings are a few. They are made of special materials. If lightning hits them, they trap the charge on the outside.

An **electric current** forms when charge flows. Electrons move from atom to atom. A **conductor**, like metal, helps them move. The charge flows through wires. This path is called a **circuit**.

Insulators stop the flow. Glass, wood, plastic, air, and rubber are a few. Wires are wrapped in insulators. This prevents shocks.

wires
insulator

CHAPTER 3

HOW IS ELECTRICITY MADE?

How does electricity get to your home? It often comes from a power plant.

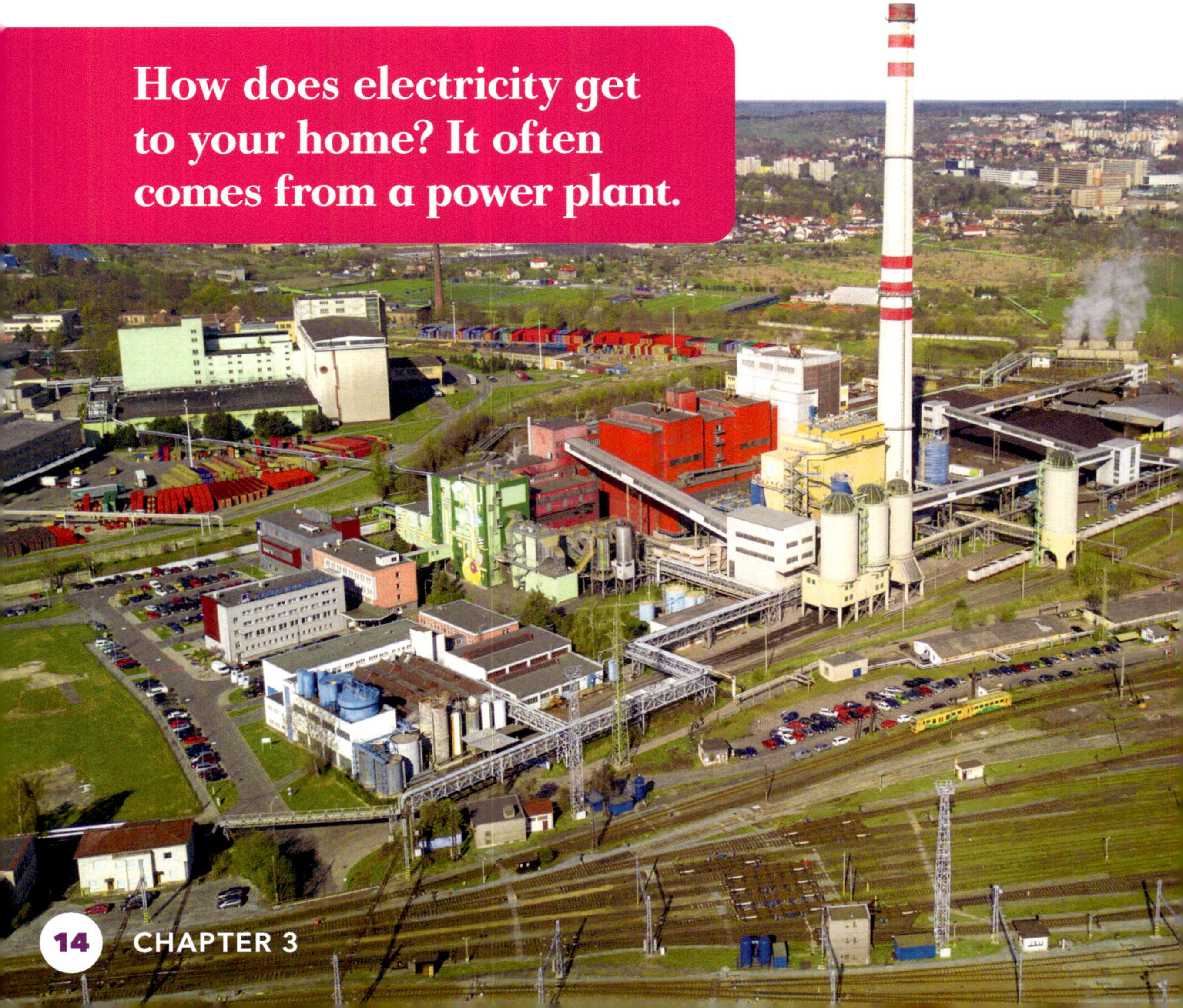

Power plants start with an **energy** source. Most power plants burn **fossil fuels**. These include coal, gas, and oil. Others use **nuclear reactions**. Some power plants use water or wind power. Wind turbines turn wind energy into electricity.

Energy turns fans. Fans start a **generator**. In it, wires wrap around an electric magnet. The magnet moves. It pushes charge through the wires. Electric current flows to your home! How? It travels through power lines.

TAKE A LOOK!

How does a generator turn energy into an electric current? Take a look!

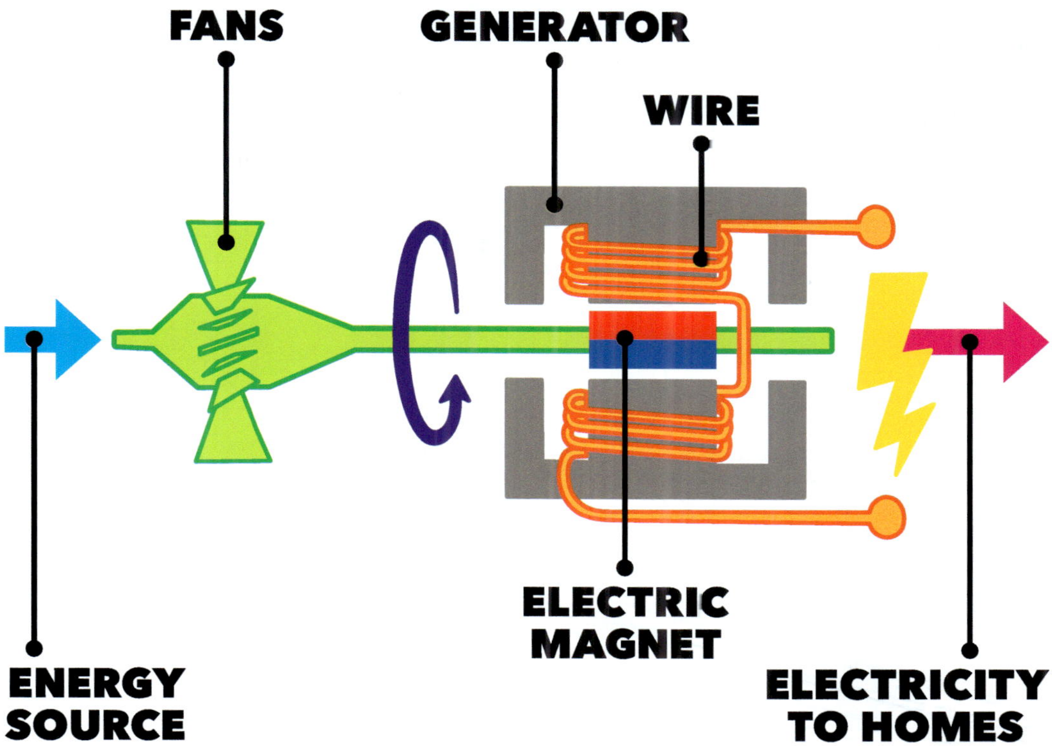

Some things need more power. Others need less. A **watt** measures how fast something uses energy. A laptop uses 30 watts. A refrigerator uses 1400 watts.

A **volt** shows how strong the power is. Many wall outlets are 120 volts. Lightning can have one billion volts!

DID YOU KNOW?

A meter on your home measures the amount of watts your household uses. The power company checks the meter. They send you a bill based on how much you use.

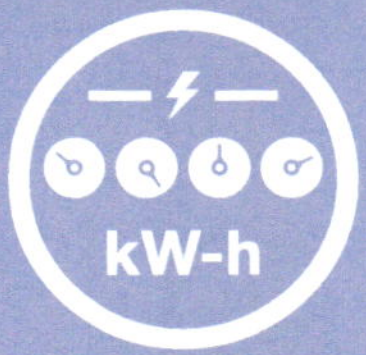

A lot happens to power everything in your home. What are some ways you use electricity?

ACTIVITIES & TOOLS

TRY THIS!

MAKE STATIC ELECTRICITY

Make static electricity on your own with this activity. You will need to do this on a dry day.

What You Need:

- plastic spoon
- salt
- plate
- paper towel
- ruler
- spices
- small pieces of paper

1. **Pour one spoonful of salt onto a plate.**
2. **Rub the empty spoon with the paper towel 10 times.**
3. **Hold the spoon just above the salt. Do not let the spoon and salt touch. Does the salt jump to the spoon?**
4. **Repeat Step 2.**
5. **Now hold the spoon one inch above the salt. Does the salt jump to the spoon? Is it less salt, more, or the same amount as before?**
6. **Repeat Steps 4 and 5 a few times, raising the spoon one inch higher each time. Does less salt stick to the spoon each time? Try this until no more salt sticks.**
7. **Try this with spices or small pieces of paper. Do these stick to the spoon like the salt did? Why do you think this is?**

GLOSSARY

appliances: Machines that do particular jobs, such as driers, toasters, or blenders.

atoms: The tiniest parts of elements that have all the properties of their elements.

charge: A part of an atom that makes something stick or push away.

circuit: A complete path for an electric current.

conductor: A substance that allows heat, electricity, or sound to travel through it.

electric current: The flow of charge from atom to atom.

electricity: A form of energy caused by the motion of electrons.

electrons: Tiny particles that move around the nuclei of atoms and carry negative electrical charges.

energy: The resources used to produce power.

fossil fuels: Coal, oil, or natural gas, formed from the remains of prehistoric plants and animals.

generator: A machine that produces electricity by turning a magnet inside a coil of wire.

insulators: Materials that block the flow of heat, electricity, or sound.

nuclear reactions: The actions of splitting apart or joining parts of atoms.

volt: A unit for measuring the force of an electric current or the stored power of a battery.

watt: A unit for measuring electrical power.

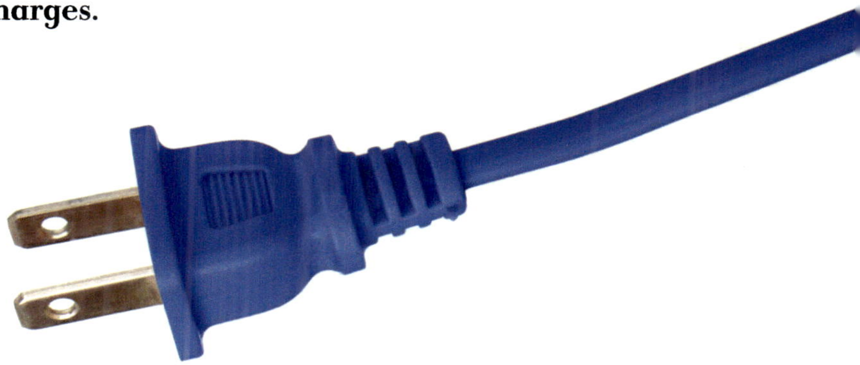

INDEX

TO LEARN MORE

Finding more information is as easy as 1, 2, 3.

1. Go to www.factsurfer.com
2. Enter "electricity" into the search box.
3. Choose your book to see a list of websites.

FACT SURFER